THE LITTLE BOOK OF TRAVEL TIPS

MEGAN DEVENISH

THE LITTLE BOOK OF TRAVEL TIPS

MEGAN DEVENISH

A.
Absolute Press

First published in Great Britain in 2007 by
Absolute Press
Scarborough House, 29 James Street West
Bath BA1 2BT, England
Phone 44 (0) 1225 316013 **Fax** 44 (0) 1225 445836
E-mail info@absolutepress.co.uk
Web www.absolutepress.co.uk

A catalogue record of this book is available from the British Library

ISBN 13: 9781904573647

Printed and bound in Italy by Legoprint

'I travel not to go anywhere, but to go.
I travel for travel's sake.
The great affair is to move.'

Robert Louis Stevenson

1

When buying train or bus tickets, always make the effort to **write the destination, ticket type and travel date in the native language** before approaching the ticket counters.

2

Prepare for the worst.

Make several copies of your passport. Leave one copy at home with a friend and keep the other with you in a place separate from your passport.

3

Driving abroad?

Ensure that your car is ready and study the local road conditions, laws and other driving requirements. Also, remember to take with you the vehicle registration documents and your motor insurance certificate.

4

Check the dates of local major holidays and festivals.

Public services may be limited on these dates and you might have to allow extra time for travel.

5

Before you go, **e-mail yourself a copy of all your important information**

such as flight references and phone numbers and details for your credit cards, passport and driving licence. If you should then happen to lose your documents or have your wallet stolen, you need only to log on to access your details.

6

Proof of immunisation against certain diseases **is a requirement before entering some countries,** so always check with a doctor before leaving lest this be the case.

7

Pack essentials

such as toothbrush, clean underwear and money **in your hand luggage**

in case your check-in bags get lost. That way you can stay clean and afford to eat until your bags turn up!

8

Learn local graces.

Having an awareness of social etiquette will give you a greater insight into a country's culture and will gain you respect – and possibly favour and enhanced service – from the people.

9

Read the small print on your travel insurance and check exactly what you're covered for before taking part in any activities that may render it void and leave you in a sticky situation.

10

If withdrawing money from an ATM, try to **use a machine outside a bank** and make sure the bank is open. That way if the machine eats your card you should be able go inside and retrieve it.

11

Never leave home without first researching the visa requirements

for your choice of country. Find out how long the visa lasts and check that you have the right type for your stay.

12

Perfect Packing No.1:

If you travel frequently it can be useful to

duplicate all toiletry items,

such as hairbrush, razor, toothbrush and shampoo. It will make packing and unpacking faster and easier.

13

If you're serious about saving money

check air fares often. Air fare prices fluctuate regularly so it's worth checking them every day, even two or three times a day to ensure the best deal.

14

If away for longer than a month and leaving your mobile at home **change your phone tariff to the lowest possible line rental** option to avoid large bills.

15

Perfect Packing No.2: Roll rather than fold clothes.

This will prevent wrinkles. It will also help to create more space.

16

Before you go, contact your mobile phone company to **check that your phone will work abroad**

...and then remember to take your charger!

17

Take an alarm clock

or a watch with an alarm function away with you. It will always be useful but especially so for getting you to the airport on time!

18

Travelling with Children No.1: Make safety tags for each young child.

This should be a card which states their name, the place they are staying, a contact phone number and their parents' or carers' names. If you should become separated, this could help you find a missing child.

19

Secure luggage with a combination lock instead of a padlock. It avoids any risk of losing tiny keys during your trip.

20

It's always useful to **figure out the local tipping custom before you go.**

This should save embarrassment and make life far easier.

21

Be sure to

return your hire car with a full tank of fuel

to avoid any extra, and probably unreasonable, costs imposed by the rental company.

22

Perfect Packing No.3: Keep medicines in their original packaging;

it will help airport security to identify what you have, and will avoid delays or confiscations at customs.

23

Always **label your luggage clearly on the outside and on the inside** to avoid confusion if the outer label gets stripped off.

24

Ask your bed and breakfast **host or locals to recommend** special attractions and activities that are free or low-cost rather than booking expensive tours.

25

Make a note of any severe **allergies** you may have **and put it in your wallet.**

It will be even more useful written in the language of the country you are visiting.

26

Make copies of your travellers' cheques before you go.

Keep the copies and make a note of the serial number of each, the denominations and the date and location of their purchase.

27

Travelling with Children No.2

Try to **choose an airline that is child-friendly.**

Some airlines, even the discount carriers, will make special allowances for families.

28

Before you depart, **find out whether there is a departure tax,** and how much it is. Some countries do charge a small fee and will not let you board your flight without first paying it. Also, be sure to reserve cash for these taxes as not all countries will accept credit cards or other forms of payment.

29

Learn the language.

Even 'hello', 'please' and 'thank you' – a *bonjour* in Paris, a *bitte* in Berlin or a *gracias* in Madrid – will gain you respect from the locals and make your trip easier.

30

Be flexible, if possible, with where you fly to and from.

Choosing a nearby or secondary airport for your departure or arrival can save a lot of money.

31

Print a currency conversion table that will fit into your wallet for quick, easy and discreet reference.

32

Make sure the emergency page in your passport is up to date and that all the required details are correct. You never know when this information could be crucial.

33

When booking flights,

ask if there is a surcharge for booking on the telephone rather than online before you make your reservation.

34

Avoid hanging the ‘Please Clean Room’ tag on your door.

It is an obvious signal that you are not in and leaves you vulnerable to theft.

35

Travelling with Children No.3: Carry a recent picture of your child with you at all times. If you get separated it will help you to more quickly locate your child.

36

Inform your bank before you travel to ensure there won't be any difficulties when using your credit and debit cards abroad. The unfamiliar spending patterns might cause them to suspect that the card is being used fraudulently.

37

If you get into trouble, contact

the nearest **embassy**

for your country. Many of them

will provide some level of assistance in an emergency.

38

Tired of queuing? Check to **see if your airline has an online check-in facility** to minimise the time you spend at the airport.

39

Wherever you are going you should **always check travel warnings issued by the government or state.** If you happen to be travelling to areas where there is conflict, war or violence, this information could just save your life.

40

Bad weather or schedule delays can lead to long waits or cancellations. You could be held up for a long time (and might need to sleepover).

An emergency airport survival kit

could include: eye shades; ear plugs; cash to see you OK for food and drink; books, magazines or a personal stereo to keep you entertained; a pillow or surrogate; some toilet paper and disinfectant wipes (not all airports will be well-stocked and clean) and an alarm clock or watch (to ensure you don't miss the next flight!).

41

Get an Upgrade No.1: Be subtle; be discreet.

It's highly unlikely that staff will upgrade you with other customers within earshot.

42

Try taking vitamin B before you go to a mosquito-infested country as this should help **to reduce the risk of being bitten.** Alternatively, buy a repellent with a high 'deet' content. This is the active ingredient in most insect repellents and is usually highly effective.

43

US dollars are often **a very useful form of currency to carry,** especially if travelling to the developing world where they are widely recognised and accepted.

44

Try and **use reduced-rate phone cards to call home** instead of pricey hotel phones. They are usually easy to purchase and are far better value for money.

45

Make sure your passport does not expire within 6 months

of your date **of travel.**

A large majority of countries insist that your passport be valid for at least that time period.

46

To reduce jet lag going westward,

(such as London to New York), get lots of bright natural light in the early evenings before you go as this will help you to adapt to New York time.

47

To reduce jet lag going eastward,

(back to the UK from the US), try and return at around midday to get the brightest light of the day.

48

Get an Upgrade No.2: Join a frequent flier programme.

They're completely free to sign up to and, usually, you'll be given priority over economy ticket holders when upgrades are available or necessary.

49

Every doctor's surgery has guidelines of which vaccinations you need to take for which part of the world, so always **check** far **in advance** what type of **diseases** are **common to the area** you'll be visiting.

50

Get an Upgrade No.3: Let staff know about any special occasion, such as your honeymoon. It can be useful to take your marriage certificate with you to prove it.

Megan Devenish

Megan Devenish's mother insists that her daughter was first bitten by the travel bug at the tender age of 3. Since then she's been bitten by sandflies in New Zealand, been hissed at by snakes in the Australian rainforest and been spat at by camels in Tunisia. She's roughed it in fifty-rupee Rajasthani shacks. She's camped along the Serbian left bank of the Danube. She's traversed by tuk-tuk, canoe, ski and blistered foot. She has fallen asleep to countless Greyhound engine hums, under the starlit skies shared by the Karpathion Sea and in the slightly less romantic and stellar confines of London's Heathrow Airport.

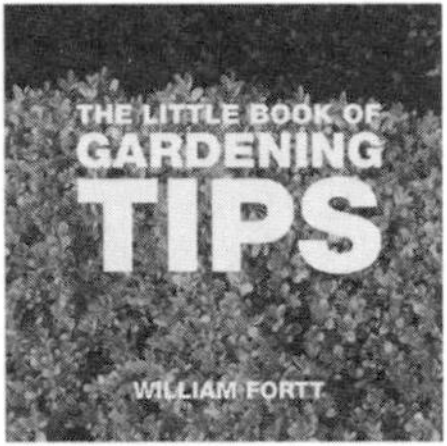

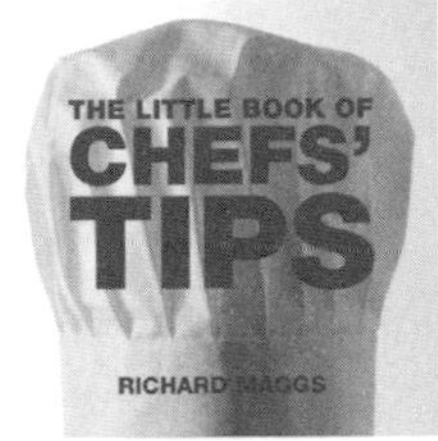

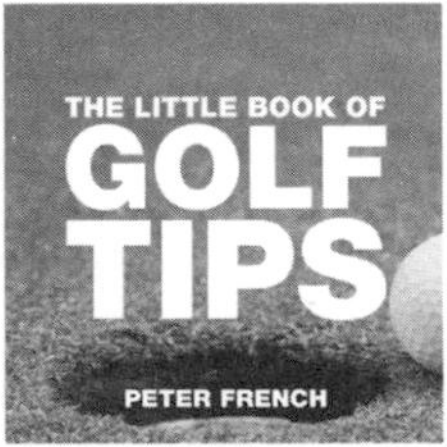

THE LITTLE BOOK OF

TIPS SERIES

THE LITTLE BOOK OF
CHEESE
TIPS
ANDREW LANGLEY

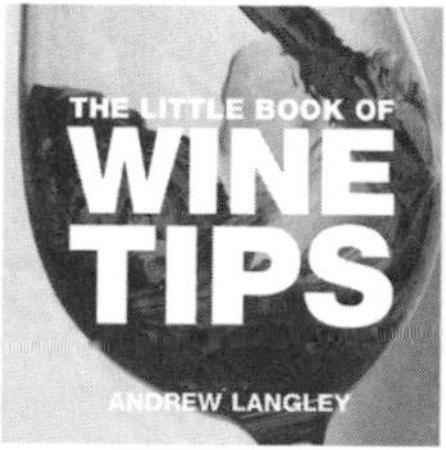
THE LITTLE BOOK OF
WINE
TIPS
ANDREW LANGLEY

THE LITTLE BOOK OF
AGA
TIPS²
RICHARD MAGGS

THE LITTLE BOOK OF
COFFEE
TIPS
ANDREW LANGLEY

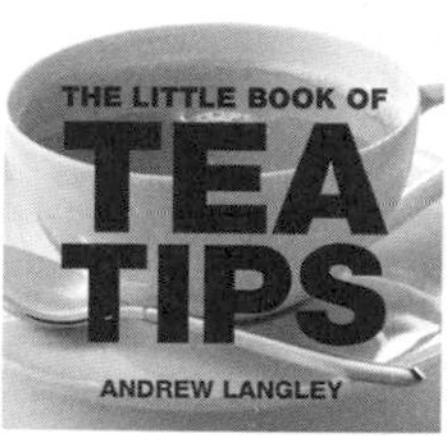
THE LITTLE BOOK OF
TEA
TIPS
ANDREW LANGLEY

THE LITTLE BOOK OF
AGA
TIPS³
RICHARD MAGGS

THE LITTLE BOOK OF
AGA
TIPS
RICHARD MAGGS

THE LITTLE BOOK OF
CHRISTMAS
AGA
TIPS
RICHARD MAGGS

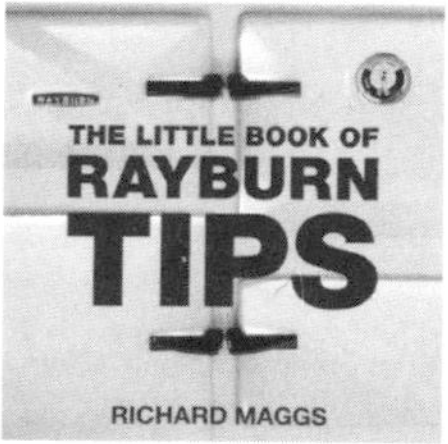
THE LITTLE BOOK OF
RAYBURN
TIPS
RICHARD MAGGS

THE LITTLE BOOK OF
BRIDGE
TIPS
PETER FRENCH

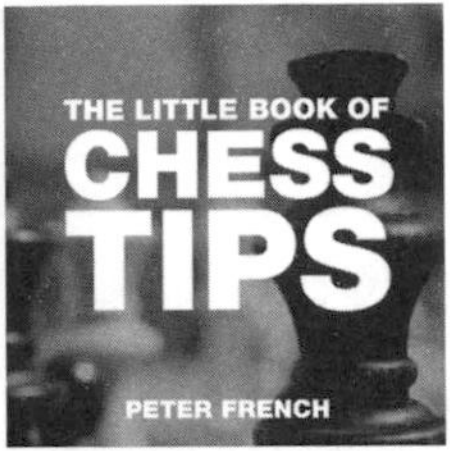
THE LITTLE BOOK OF
CHESS
TIPS
PETER FRENCH

THE LITTLE BOOK OF
FISHING
TIPS
HAEL DEVENISH

THE LITTLE BOOK OF
GREEN
TIPS
WILLIAM FORTT

THE LITTLE BOOK OF
KITTEN
TIPS
ANDREW LANGLEY

MARMITE
PAUL HARTLEY
THE LITTLE BOOK OF
MARMITE
TIPS

THE LITTLE BOOK OF
PUPPY
TIPS
ANDREW LANGLEY

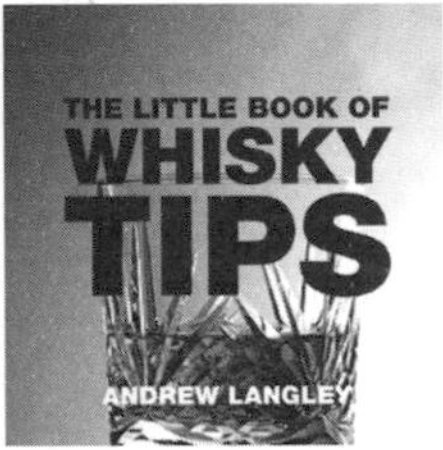
THE LITTLE BOOK OF
WHISKY
TIPS
ANDREW LANGLEY

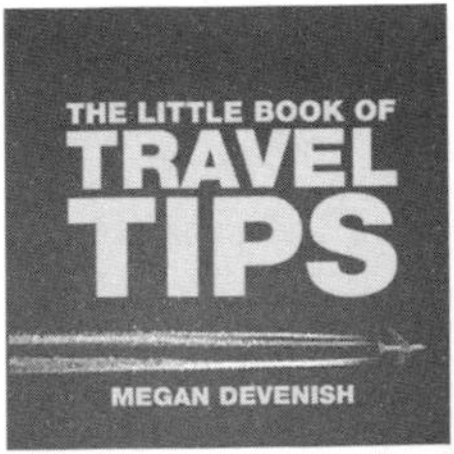
THE LITTLE BOOK OF
TRAVEL
TIPS
MEGAN DEVENISH

Little Books of Tips from Absolute Press

Tea Tips
Wine Tips
Cheese Tips
Coffee Tips
Herb Tips
Gardening Tips
Barbecue Tips
Chefs' Tips
Spice Tips
Beer Tips
Poker Tips

Golf Tips
Aga Tips
Aga Tips 2
Aga Tips 3
Christmas Aga Tips
Rayburn Tips
Puppy Tips
Kitten Tips
Travel Tips
Fishing Tips
Marmite Tips

All titles: £2.99 / 112 pages

Forthcoming Titles:

Green Tips
Whisky Tips
Bridge Tips
Chess Tips